# USING BLOOM'S TAXONOMY TO WRITE EFFECTIVE LEARNING OBJECTIVES

The ABCDs of Writing Learning Objectives: A Basic Guide

Edmund Bilon

# CONTENTS

# LEARNING OBJECTIVES

Learning objectives identify what students should know or be able to do at the end of an instructional unit. These desired results should influence the choice of topics, how much content to include, and the sequencing of those topics. Learning objectives describe the knowledge and skills we want students to gain from our instruction. In addition to letting students know what they must do to successfully complete your course, learning objectives are used to:

- Communicate our intentions clearly to students and to colleagues.
- Provide a framework for selecting and organizing course content.
- Guide decisions about assessment and evaluation methods.
- Provide a framework for selecting appropriate teaching and learning activities.
- Give students information for directing their learning efforts and monitoring their own progress.

Learning objectives help anchor assessments and activities in evidence-based course design. By aligning objectives, assessments, and activities, we can collect data on student performance in achieving those objectives. This information helps students and instructors to monitor student progress. At a broader level, student performance data helps learning scientists to improve theories of learning, which in turn helps learning engineers to make interactive improvements to the course.

Creating concise objectives is key to developing purposeful and systematic instruction. One of the most prevalent conclusions that educators have drawn from the large body of instructional research is that instruction needs to be tailored to support concrete instructional objectives and to meet specific learning outcomes.[1]

**Primary purposes of learning objectives?**

- Articulate learning objectives so students know what is expected of them. Explicitly articulated objectives are essential because students must know what is expected of them in order to achieve the goals of a course.
- Provide information that helps them set priorities and monitor their own progress. Objectives provide information that helps students set priorities and monitor their own progress.
- Provide a framework for selecting and organizing instructional content. Online course development is often a team effort involving instructional designers, graphic designers, video producers, and others who must collaborate to produce consistent, cohesive content and activities. Objectives provide a framework for selecting and organizing instructional content for the diverse professionals involved in a collaborative course design project.
- Facilitate the development and use of accurate assessment tools and instructional activities. A primary consideration when writing learning objectives is whether you can assess what you are asking students to do.
- Communicate intentions and expectations. Finally, for students, well-written learning objectives help communicate the intentions and expectations of their instructors.

# THE DIFFERENCE BETWEEN A GOAL AND AN OBJECTIVE

The first thing to ask yourself when developing your course is: What are your overall course goals? It's important to distinguish between the Course Goals and Student Learning Objectives. COURSE goals are the overarching goals of the class as a whole. Think about what your students should get out of the course and try to paraphrase it into a few overall course goals.

The specific TASKS of how the students will attain those course goals will be described within the Student Learning Objectives of a module or a unit. Here is an example of an Overall Course Goal from a Journalism course. It reads, "Examine ethical dilemmas facing media professionals across the disciplines of advertising, journalism, public relations, and communication. "HOW the students will examine those ethical dilemmas will be described in more detail within the Student Learning Objectives for each module. For example, one module of this course might focus on the ethical dilemmas in ADVERTISING, while an entirely separate module might focus on the journalism dilemma – and so on.

The goals of a course or unit of instruction are stated in various ways and in various places, such as in course descriptions and topic lists used in course catalogs and other introductory material. Phrases such as "you will be able to" and "students will gain insight into" often pepper these materials and sometimes may be confused with learning objectives because of the similar wording. However, course descriptions and topics lists tell learners what to expect of the course, whereas learning objectives tell learners what is expected of them. Consider the following statement from the course description of Carnegie Mellon University's Open Learning Initiative (OLI) Introduction to Psychology course:

> *Throughout this study of human behavior and the mind, you will gain insight into the history of the field of psychology, as well as explore current theories and issues in areas such as cognition, motivation, and wellness.*

Similar to a learning objective, this goal describes desirable results of completing the course. However, although it tells students what they will gain from completing the course, it does not tell them what they must do to achieve the desirable results. Consequently, this statement fails to provide students with a concrete way to demonstrate mastery of a skill—which is an important function of a learning objective.

- **goal**—the end toward which effort is directed
- **objective**—something toward which effort is directed

Despite their synonymous relationship, goal and objective have different meanings in the context of education and instruction. Instructors need to understand the fine distinctions between their use so that they can develop clear objectives based on the goals of the course.

Goals state, in general terms, the aims or purposes of instruction. They are often stated as broad, long-range outcomes that instruction is intended to achieve rather than as observable or measurable actions. Well-considered goals provide a basis on which detailed learning objectives can be developed: you can analyze a goal to identify the knowledge and skills necessary to achieve the goal, then state the knowledge and skills as learning objectives.

Objectives state, in precise terms, the intended learning outcomes of a unit of instruction. The primary difference between a goal and an objective is that an objective specifies observable and/or measurable skills and knowledge that students must demonstrate to show achievement of the broader goals.

# EXAMPLES OF GOAL STATEMENTS AND LEARNING OBJECTIVES

The following goal statement is for a course on electronic health record systems:

- Learners will understand the importance of electronic health record use in public health.

The goal is broad, but it provides guidance in writing observable, measurable learning objectives such as the following:

- Learners will list four ways that electronic health records are used to support public health.
- Learners will explain how patient confidentiality is protected when records are shared with public health agencies.
- Learners will describe the process of de-identifying protected health information.

The following table summarizes the differences between goals and objectives.

|  | Goal | Objective |
|---|---|---|
| Term | Long term | Short term |
| Applicability | Generic across course | Specific to units of instruction |

| Size and scope | Large | Small or medium |
|---|---|---|
| Measure | Not specifically measurable | Observable and/ or measurable |
| Increments and steps | Not stated | Incremented according to achievement of previous objectives |

**Knowledge Check**

Determine whether the following is a goal or an objective.

1.  A nurse will demonstrate how to scan a patient's barcoded wristband to confirm proper patient identification.
    a.  Goal
    b.  Objective
2.  Strive to grow membership annually at XYZ gym.
    a.  Goal
    b.  Objective
3.  Radiology technicians will be able to demonstrate the 5-step process for archiving a medical image in the EHR system.
    a.  Goal
    b.  Objective
4.  Develop an increased understanding of careers in health education by the end of the Fall 2016 semester.
    a.  Goal
    b.  Objective

**Answers:**

1.  Objective: Objectives use terms that are specific and measurable. A nurse can clearly demonstrate how to scan a patient's barcode and display his medication profile.
2.  Goal: This statement is a goal. It is very broad and

nonspecific. For example, it does not state how much membership needs to grow, so it would be hard to tell whether membership increased, and the goal was achieved at the end of a year.

3.    Objective: This is an objective. Demonstrating the process for archiving a medical image is a specific, observable, and measurable action.

4.    Goal: This statement is a goal. We cannot know how much of an increase demonstrates success, and we cannot observe or measure understanding.

# THE DIFFERENCE BETWEEN A COURSE DESCRIPTION, A TOPICS LIST, AND AN OBJECTIVE

Every course has learning objectives, whether stated in writing or implied, and instructors are often asked to present those objectives for purposes such as developing promotional materials or having the course accepted by an institution. Instructors who rely on implicit objectives sometimes misunderstand the request for learning objectives and instead submit a course description or a list of topics. For those instructors, the course description and topics list may signify their implicit objectives. However, neither course descriptions nor topics lists provide the specificity or precision of learning objectives that include the four key elements: audience, behavior, condition, and degree. Consequently, neither can provide the same kind of support to course development or student metacognition.

Course descriptions and topics lists are used primarily for promotional materials. They provide students and others a broad view of what a course is about and what topics it covers. Learning objectives have a very different purpose. They are statements that guide students in their learning efforts from the beginning to the end of the course, and they describe what students must do to demonstrate mastery of each objective.

As you have learned, learning objectives must clearly state expectations to students; guide instructors in selecting course content, learning activities, and assessment methods; provide a means to direct learning efforts and monitor progress; build a framework for collecting student performance data; and align with course activities and assessments. Creating objectives that can perform such heavy lifting may seem like a daunting task, but in the Implementation module, we provide tips and guidelines to help you develop solid objectives-writing skills. We also present the ABCD approach to writing learning objectives, which simplifies the process of creating thorough, effective objectives.

**Knowledge Check**

True or false? Objectives state several results that students can expect from the course using terms that sound much like "Students will explore..." and "Students will learn...."
   A. True
   B. False

**Answer:** False: Course descriptions, not learning objectives, state several results that students can expect from the course using terms that sound much like "Students will explore..." and "Students will learn...."

# CHARACTERISTICS OF AN EFFECTIVE LEARNING OBJECTIVE: ABCD APPROACH TO WRITING LEARNING OBJECTIVES

Creating learning objectives, like many tasks, can be simplified if you have a process or formula to follow. The ABCD approach to instructional objectives is a tool that provides just that—a formula, or template, that helps you create thorough and effective objectives. The ABCD approach specifies four key characteristics that contribute to effective learning objectives:

1. audience,
2. behavior,
3. condition,
4. and degree.

The audience is the learner who will demonstrate the behavior under specified conditions and to an acceptable degree. The behavior—what the learner is expected to be able to do—must be observable and/or measurable. The condition, if any, describes the circumstances under which the learner will exhibit the behavior. The degree, if applicable, states the criterion for acceptable performance.

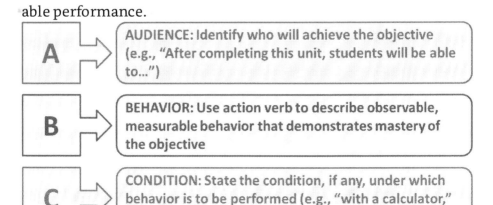

The following examples diagram two learning objectives and demonstrate two noteworthy points. Example 1 shows that not every learning objective must contain a condition or state a degree.

## Example 1

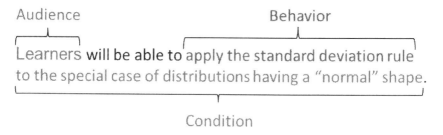

Example 2 shows that the ABCDs do not have to be in a particular order.

## Example 2

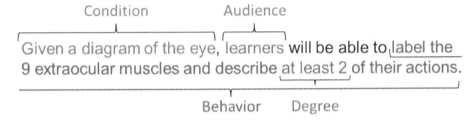

# DEVELOPING YOUR LEARNING OBJECTIVES: AUDIENCE

What *prior knowledge* do students bring to your course? Prior knowledge is the combination of a learner's preexisting attitudes, experiences, and knowledge. By carefully considering prior knowledge and recognizing its value as building blocks for new knowledge, you can support meaningful learning with a strong foundation of accurate information. You should design your course around what students will be able to do and avoid teaching what they already know. If you are unsure about what prior knowledge students bring with them into the course, you can design pre-course assessments to evaluate their prior knowledge and adjust your learning objectives, course assessments, activities, and instructional approaches as needed.

Accurate understandings are referred to as prior knowledge, and inaccurate understandings are referred to as misconceptions. Understanding both the prior knowledge and misconceptions that students hold is critical to your objective design. The first step in making prior knowledge work for you and your students is to determine what your students know and what misconceptions they have, what they believe they know, and what they need to know.

The better you understand your audience—their prior knowledge, goals and motivations, values, attitudes, and other factors that influence their learning—the better you can tailor your learning objectives to meet their needs. Keeping your audience's perspective in mind as you develop your learning objectives helps ensure that your objectives are relevant, student centered, and focused on what students must achieve to successfully complete your course. As you are thinking about your course design, you cannot know exactly what prior knowledge students have, so you must identify the learning objectives and skills students need to successfully complete your course.

Once you have identified your audience with these factors in mind, writing the audience part of the ABCDs is simple. Learning objectives commonly begin with a phrase such as "After reviewing this section, students will be able to..." or "After completing this activity, learners will be able to..." Repeating opening phrases in a list of objectives, however, is redundant. A commonly used alternative is to name the audience in an introductory sentence before the list of objectives, as in the following figure.

After reviewing this page, students will be able to do the following:
- Name the phases of mitosis
- Explain the process of mitosis
- Sketch the progression of mitosis in a five-stage diagram

Audience is identified in an introductory paragraph

Another way to avoid repetition is to imply the audience by simply listing the objectives under a heading. The implied audience know who they are—the important point of the audience element is that you understand who they are.

Audience is implied and
objectives are listed under
a heading

**Learning Objectives**
- Name the phases of mitosis
- Explain the process of mitosis
- Sketch the progression of mitosis
  in a five-stage diagram

Although the students had factual and perhaps conceptual knowledge, the gap resulted from lack of procedural knowledge (see Behavior and Bloom's Taxonomy)—they could not synthesize their factual knowledge with the conceptual knowledge needed to apply it. The reverse is also true: knowing how to perform a particular task does not necessarily mean a person understands the underlying concepts of the task. It is important not to assume that because students have one kind of knowledge, they also have another. Knowing your audience, particularly the prior knowledge they bring to your course, is a critical element to help you ensure that students have a strong foundation that promotes meaningful learning.

## Example: Keep Learning Objectives Student Centered

Learning objectives are a powerful tool for you, but their primary purpose is to tell students what they must do to successfully complete your course. The following is an instructor-centered, not student-centered, objective, and it describes an instructional activity rather than the knowledge or skill students must demonstrate after this activity:

- Arrange for a U.S. Fish and Wildlife Service representative to speak to the class about endangered species.

Here is a student-centered learning objective related to the instructional activity. It specifically states what is expected of the students:

- Students will describe the role of the U.S. Fish and Wildlife service in protecting endangered species in the

United States.

**Knowledge Check**
1.  Which of the following describes prior knowledge? Select all that apply.
>  a.   Prior knowledge is unchanging and is re-
tained forever.
>  b.   Prior knowledge is the combination of a
learner's preexisting attitudes, experiences,
and knowledge.
>  c.   It is critical to assess both the amount
and nature of students' prior knowledge.
>  d.   Students often believe all of their prior
knowledge is accurate, but sometimes what
students perceive to be knowledge is actually
a misconception.

2.  Which of the following objectives are student
centered? Select all that apply.
>  a.   Provide an introduction to the field of
robotics.
>  b.   Cover three theories of child develop-
ment.
>  c.   Perform wildlife disease risk analysis
using the 5-step model outlined by Jacob-
Hoff and colleagues.
>  d.   Compare and contrast Erikson's, Piaget's,
and Vygotsky's theories of child development.

**Answer:**
1.  b, c and d: Prior knowledge is the combination
of a learner's preexisting attitudes, experiences,
and knowledge. Also, it is critical to assess both the
amount and nature of students' prior knowledge so

that we can design our instruction appropriately. Additionally, sometimes students' understandings are accurate, providing a foundation for building new knowledge, and sometimes they are inaccurate. Accurate understandings are referred to as prior knowledge, and inaccurate understandings are referred to as misconceptions.

2.    c and d: These objectives focus on what students should do.

# DEVELOPING YOUR LEARNING OBJECTIVES: BEHAVIOR (1 OF 3)

# BEHAVIOR

The behavior described in a learning objective must clearly state an *observable and/or measurable* action that students can perform to demonstrate mastery of the skill or knowledge called for by the objective. It requires precise language that students can interpret without ambiguity.

Bloom's taxonomy provides a rich source of action verbs that can help you compose observable and/or measurable objectives that align with assessments. Bloom's taxonomy is a classification system of intellectual behaviors—thinking, learning, understanding—developed as a means to measure proficiency and competence. The taxonomy was developed by a team of cognitive

psychologists, led by Dr. Benjamin Bloom, in an effort to make assessment more systematic and to promote higher levels of thinking in education, such as analysis and evaluation rather than just restating facts.

# DOMAINS OF BLOOM'S TAXONOMY

Individually and collectively, people possess widely varying knowledge and skills as well as different levels of expertise. Consider, for example, the differences in the following skills:

- Performing surgery
- Dancing with a ballet troupe
- Editing an article for a professional journal
- Developing a detailed outline for a training activity
- Convincing a group to buy a product or service
- Mediating a dispute between co-workers

Bloom's taxonomy of educational objectives is a framework for classifying different ways of thinking about and ordering objectives. According to Bloom [2], learning occurs in three domains: cognitive, affective, and psychomotor.

Bloom and his colleagues recognized the need to classify knowledge and skills in order to be able to assess them. They identified three domains of learning activity: The *cognitive* domain addresses knowledge and thinking skills such as writing an essay. The *psychomotor* domain encompasses physical skills such as manipulating a tool or an instrument. The *affective* domain is concerned with subjective areas such as emotional development and conflict resolution. Bloom's domains are sometimes listed with word associations to make them easier to remember:

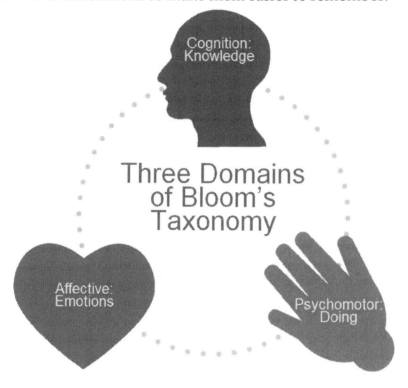

The three domain are sometimes collectively called **KSA** for *knowledge* (cognitive domain), *skills* (psychomotor domain), and *attitude* (affective domain). KSA is often used in government training documents and websites and refers to the requirements for given jobs through qualified work experience, training, and education. Over time, the original version has evolved, and modified versions have been published. [3],[4]

**Knowledge Check**

1. Which of the following is an example of a learning objective in the affective domain?
    a. Create a detailed outline for a training activity.
    b. Perform with a ballet troupe.
    c. Mediate a dispute between co-workers.
    d. Edit an article for a journal.

2. Which of the following is an example of a learning objective in the psychomotor domain?
    a. Given a pair of cut lenses from a nonstock frame, assemble a pair of eyeglasses.
    b. Distinguish the types of logical fallacy that undermine an argument's form.
    c. Formulate an argument that is counter to your own opinion of a controversial issue.
    d. Propose an action plan that generates support for a cause that is important to you.

3. Which of the following is an example of a learning objective in the cognitive domain?
    a. Measure the spherical, cylindrical, and axis values of eyeglass lenses using a manual lensometer.
    b. Manipulate the colonoscope during a colonoscopy.
    c. Categorize criminal activity according to whether it is a personal, property, inchoate, or statutory crime.
    d. Take a stand for or against a controversial social issue and justify your position.

Answers:

1. c: "Mediating" is what makes this an affective skill; it encompasses the way individuals act or react emotionally.

2. a: "Assembling a pair of eyeglasses" is what distinguishes this learning objective as being in the

psychomotor domain. Learning objectives written for the psychomotor domain entail learning new skills or altering or combining existing skills that involve physical ability and manual dexterity.

3.   c: "Categorize" is what distinguishes this objective as being in the cognitive domain. The cognitive domain focuses on intellectual skills that are categorized according to cognitive complexity.

# COGNITIVE DOMAIN

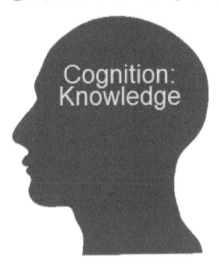

The revised Bloom's taxonomy divides the *cognitive* domain into a cognitive process dimension and a *knowledge* dimension [5], [6]. The cognitive process dimension involves the development of intellectual skills, which are categorized along a continuum of cognitive complexity from lower-order to higher-order thinking skills: remember, understand, apply, analyze, evaluate, and create.

| Cognitive Level | Description | Verbs Commonly Used in Cognitive Objectives |
|---|---|---|
| Remembering | Retrieving and recalling relevant knowledge from long-term memory | Recall, identify |
| Understanding | Constructing meaning | Interpret, exemplify, |

| | from oral, written, and graphic messages through interpreting, exemplifying, classifying, summarizing, inferring, comparing, and explaining | classify, summarize, infer, compare, explain |
|---|---|---|
| Applying | Carrying out or using a procedure through executing or implementing; applying knowledge to actual situations | Execute, implement, relate, sketch |
| Analyzing | Breaking material into constituent parts; determining how the parts relate to one another and to an overall structure or purpose through differentiating, organizing, and attributing | Differentiate, organize, attribute, select |
| Evaluating | Making judgments based on criteria and standards through checking and critiquing | Assess, check, critique, predict |
| Creating | Putting elements together to form a coherent or functional whole; re-organizing elements into a new pattern or structure through generating, planning, or producing | Generate, plan, produce |

## Examples of Cognitive Objectives

Remember

- Students will be able to identify mitosis.
- Students will be able to name the phases of mitosis.

Understand

- Students will be able to define mitosis.

- Students will be able to explain the process of mitosis.
- Students will be able to summarize the central limit theorem.

Apply

- Students will be able to sketch the progression of mitosis in a five-stage diagram.
- Students will relate the law of supply and demand to the costs of health care.

Analyze

- Students will be able to compare and contrast classical conditioning and operant conditioning.
- Students will be able to select a healthy exercise plan for an overweight child.

Evaluate

- Students will be able to evaluate the George W. Bush administration's actions in conducting the 2003 U.S.-led invasion of Iraq without declaring war.
- Students will be able to assess current artificial intelligence technology and describe its potential applications in health care.

Create

- Students will be able to compose a villanelle (a poem of 19 lines with two refrains and two repeating rhymes).
- Students will be able to create a three-dimensional bump map in Adobe Photoshop.

# KNOWLEDGE DIMENSION

The knowledge dimension was added to the revised taxonomy to help you consider the types of knowledge we use:

- **Factual:** Knowledge of terminology and of specific details and elements
- **Conceptual:** Knowledge of classifications and categories; principles and generalizations; theories, models, and structures
- **Procedural:** Knowledge of subject-specific skills and algorithms, techniques, and methods; criteria for determining when to use appropriate procedures
- **Metacognitive:** Strategic knowledge; knowledge about cognitive tasks, including appropriate contextual and conditional knowledge; self-knowledge3

A simplified way to think about the difference between the knowledge and cognitive process dimensions of the cognitive domain is that the knowledge dimension identifies the types of knowledge we use, whereas the cognitive process dimension identifies six ways we use knowledge. The following table illustrates how the cognitive process and knowledge dimensions intersect.

### Revised Bloom's Taxonomy Cognitive Domain

| | | Cognitive Process Dimension | | | | |
| --- | --- | --- | --- | --- | --- | --- |
| **Knowledge Dimension** | | Remember | Understand | Apply | Analyze | Evaluate | Create |
| | Factual | List | Summarize | Classify | Order | Rank | Combine |
| | Conceptual | Describe | Interpret | Experiment | Explain | Assess | Plan |
| | Procedural | Tabulate | Predict | Calculate | Differentiate | Conclude | Compose |
| | Meta-cognitive | Appropriate use | Execute | Construct | Achieve | Action | Actualize |

### Example: Avoid False Performance

The behavior described in a learning objective is the main component of the objective. Check carefully that the behavior is observable and unambiguous. The following is "false performance,"[1] a statement that sounds like an objective but is not:

- Understand Darwin's theory of evolution.

You can drill down into this broad concept to create a concrete objective:

- Compare and contrast evolution and microevolution.

### Example: Describe Behavior, Not Performance

A common mistake in stating performance or behavior characteristic in a learning objective is to describe a teaching point, practice exercise, or some other aspect of learning activity. Such activities are intended to teach and support the learning objective. Notice in the following examples that the behaviors described are not learning objectives but rather learning activities:

- Participate in class discussion of constructivism.
- Evaluate an essay written by a peer for tone, style, purpose, and logic.

### Knowledge Check

Which of the following learning objectives describes observable behavior? Check observable or not observable.

1. Identify logical flaws in a written argument.
   a. Observable
   b. Not observable
2. Explain Newton's second law.
   a. Observable
   b. Non observable
3. Understand the U.S. stock market.
   a. Observable
   b. Non observable
4. Appreciate the historical context of the 1940s.
   a. Observable
   b. Non observable

Answers:

1. a: Identifying flaws in reasoning (logical fallacies) is an observable behavior.
2. a: Explaining a concept or idea is an observable behavior.
3. b: An instructor cannot measure or directly observe a student's understanding.
4. b: An instructor cannot measure or directly observe a student's appreciation.

# PSYCHOMOTOR DOMAIN

The psychomotor domain of Bloom's taxonomy categorizes skills at four levels: adapting, practicing, imitating, and observing. Psychomotor objectives entail learning new skills or altering or combining existing skills that involve physical ability and manual dexterity.

Online course may not present many opportunities to work with psychomotor objectives, but we still want you to know how to write them.

| Psychomotor Level | Description | Verbs Commonly Used in Cognitive Objectives |
| --- | --- | --- |
|  |  |  |

| Observing | Pay active attention to a physical event | Select, describe, detect, differentiate |
|---|---|---|
| Imitating | Copy a physical behavior | Answer, reproduce, copy, trace, grasp |
| Practicing | Practice a particular physical activity repeatedly | Fasten, measure, assemble, dismantle, stretch |
| Adapting | Make adjustments to a physical activity in an attempt to achieve perfection | Vary, reorganize, change, adjust, rearrange |

## Examples of Psychomotor Objectives

- Students will be able to assemble a pair of eyeglasses with a plastic frame and bifocal lenses adjusted to the correct segment height.
- Students will be able to bevel the edge of a glass lens and insert it into a metal frame.
- After a demonstration by the instructor, students will repeat the process of cutting a lens pattern for a non-stock eyeglass frame.
- Students will be able to describe the methods to distinguish glass from plastic lenses without tapping the lens on a hard surface.

# AFFECTIVE DOMAIN

The affective domain of Bloom's taxonomy encompasses the way individuals act or react emotionally. It focuses on subjective factors such as motivations, appreciations, values, emotions, and attitudes. The five categories under the affective domain are characterizing, organizing, valuing, responding, and receiving.

Increased research in various areas of social sciences, such as social presence, mindset, and stereotype threat, and the impact of resulting interventions on learning gain are expected to increase the need for learning objectives in the affective domain.

| Affective Level | Description | Verbs Commonly Used in Cognitive Objectives |
|---|---|---|
| Receiving | Learner is aware and receptive; otherwise, learning cannot take place | Reply, use, describe, follow, locate |
| Responding | Learner actively par- | Discuss, answer, per- |

| | | |
|---|---|---|
| | ticipates in the process. Besides being aware, the learner responds in some fashion | form, present, write |
| Valuing | Valuing identifies the value an individual associates with an object or behavior; can range from basic acceptance to a more complex commitment | Share, invite, explain, join, report, follow, justify |
| Organizing | Learner can synthesize different information and values. Values can be organized into priorities; values are compared and synthesized | Formulate, defend, prepare, arrange, integrate |
| Characterizing (internalizing) | A belief or value becomes part of the system that controls the learner's behavior | Influence, practice, perform, discriminate, propose |

## Examples of Affective Objectives

- In 400 to 500 words, students will be able to justify an opinion for or against the death penalty.
- Students will be able to mediate a mock conflict between two classmates role-playing a helpdesk support technician and a dissatisfied customer.
- Dental hygienist students will interact in a clinical setting with pediatric patients and apply the tell-show-do model for calming children.
- Students will be able to convince a group to buy a product or service.

# WRAP UP OF BLOOM'S DOMAINS

Within each domain, levels of proficiency are identified in order of increasing complexity and assume that skills are mastered at one level before the learner progresses to the next. These measures of competence help you develop concrete learning objectives and appropriate assessments. The higher the level of expertise specified by the learning objective, the more sophisticated your assessment techniques must be.

Two of the most important educational goals are "to promote retention and to promote transfer." Retention, is the ability to recall information in much the same way that it was presented. It takes place at the first level of the cognitive domain (remember) and corresponds to the observe level of the psychomotor domain and to the receive level of the affective domain. Transfer is the process of synthesizing new information with prior knowledge and applying it to other situations. It takes place at the ascending levels of the cognitive domain: (understand, apply, analyze, evaluate, and create) and corresponds to the imitate, practice, and adapt levels of the psychomotor domain and to the respond, value, organize, and characterize levels of the affective domain. Objectives that promote transfer require a bit more thought than those that promote retention.

# NOTE: WATCH OUT FOR VERBS THAT ARE NOT OBSERVABLE OR MEASURABLE

Bloom's taxonomy provides action verbs for writing good objectives, but you need to beware of verbs that are not observable or measurable. For a learning objective to give maximum structure to instruction, it should be free of vague or ambiguous words and phrases. Following are notoriously ambiguous words and phrases that should be avoided so that the intended outcome is concise and explicit.

# WORDS TO AVOID

| | | | |
|---|---|---|---|
| believe | capacity | comprehend | conceptualize |
| depth | experience | feel | hear |
| intelligence | know | listen | memorize |
| perceive | realize | recognize | see |
| self-actualize | think | understand | appreciate |

# PHRASES TO AVOID

| | | |
|---|---|---|
| acquainted with | adjusted to | anxiety |
| appreciation for | attitude of | awareness of |
| capable of | cognizant of | comprehension of |
| conscious of | enjoyment of | familiar with |
| feeling for | immaturity | insecurity |
| interest in | interested in | knowledge of |
| knowledgeable about | self-confident in | to become |
| to reduce | understanding of | |

**Knowledge Check**

Identify whether the following activities are cognitive, psychomotor, or affective:

1. Perform a peripheral vein insertion (IV insertion).
   a. Cognitive
   b. Psychomotor
   c. Affective
2. Convince a doctor to use the patient summary screen in a new electronic health records (EHR) system.

a. Cognitive
b. Psychomotor
c. Affective
3. Grade a test.
   a. Cognitive
   b. Psychomotor
   c. Affective
4. Break down a complex training task into single objectives.
   a. Cognitive
   b. Psychomotor
   c. Affective
5. Create an outline for a training module.
   a. Cognitive
   b. Psychomotor
   c. Affective
6. Remove a Foley (urinary) catheter.
   a. Cognitive
   b. Psychomotor
   c. Affective
7. Mediate a conflict between two employees.
   a. Cognitive
   b. Psychomotor
   c. Affective

Answers:
1. b: The peripheral vein insertion task is a psychomotor, or physical, activity.
2. c: Convincing a doctor to use the patient summary screen in a new EHR system falls into the affective domain.
3. a: Grading a test is a cognitive skill.
4. a: This is a cognitive task that requires analytical skills.
5. a: Creating a training outline is a cognitive skill that requires analytical analysis.

6.  b: Removing a urinary catheter requires psy-chomotor skills.

7.  c: Mediating a conflict requires skills in the affective domain. The affective domain relates to how individuals respond emotionally.

# DEVELOPING YOUR LEARNING OBJECTIVES: CONDITION AND DEGREE

# CONDITION

A condition describes (1) what a student may or may not use to demonstrate mastery of the objective and/or (2) the circumstance under which the behavior is to be performed. *Not every objective requires a condition*, but if a condition applies, be sure to specify it clearly.

Think in concrete terms when you write conditions for demonstrating mastery of an objective: What tool, prop, or special circumstance is necessary? What tool, prop, or special circumstance should be denied? What limitations must be set, or what latitude must be given?

### Example: Condition Characteristic Adds Specificity

Suppose you are teaching a theater arts class, and the topic is nonverbal performance. The first learning objective that comes to mind is

- Students will be able to create and produce a nonverbal performance.

This learning objective is workable, but it is broad. By adding a condition, you can make your learning objective more specific, so you can better focus your instruction and students can better direct their learning efforts:

- Students will be able to create and produce a nonverbal performance **incorporating various physical movement techniques.**

Now consider a learning objective for a journalism class:

- Students will be able to write newspaper articles.

This learning objective needs to be more specific because

many variables are at play in writing newspaper articles, including type of article and how information is gathered. The revised objective contains two conditions that clarify what students are supposed to do and how they are supposed to do it:

- Students will be able to write **feature** articles **using information gathered from personal interviews.**

Now let's look at an objective from a crime scene investigation class:

- Students will be able to describe a mock crime scene.

Adding a condition makes the learning objective more specific. Students now know the circumstance under which they must demonstrate the behavior, and they will not be taken by surprise when they are given only 60 seconds to study the scene:

- **After studying a mock crime scene for 60 seconds**, students will be able to describe their observations.

Be sure that any conditions stated in your learning objectives relate to the performance of the behavior, not to the instructional activities that support the objective. The following examples do not constitute conditions:

- Given a three-part lecture....
- After completing this unit....
- Given that the student has passed an introductory course....

### Knowledge Check

1. Which of the following describes the condition characteristic of an objective?
   a. The learner who will be performing the action
   b. The knowledge or skill a learner is expected to demonstrate

       c.   The situation under which the perform-
ance is to occur

       d.   The criterion of acceptable performance

2.   Which part of this learning objective is an example of a condition? *Students will be able to describe, in order from simplest to most complex, the major levels of organization in the human organism.*

       a.   "Major levels of an organization"

       b.   This learning objective contains no condition.

       c.   "Describe major levels of organization in the human organism"

       d.   "In order of simplest to most complex"

       e.   "Students"

3.   Which of the following is an example of a condition?

       a.   "With 80 percent accuracy"

       b.   "At the end of this module"

       c.   "Without the use of a calculator"

       d.   "Prior to finishing laboratory tests"

Answers:

1.   c: An objective describes the important conditions (if any) under which the performance is to occur. Example conditions include "working with a partner," "without the use of a calculator," and "given a CPR manikin."

2.   d: The condition is "in order of simplest to most complex"

3.   c: "Without the use of a calculator" is a condition: the student is being asked to perform a task without the use of a calculator.

# DEGREE

Learning objectives sometimes state a degree of acceptable performance. Often, the degree is implied; that is, students can assume the behavior is to be performed without error unless a criterion is explicitly stated. In other cases, the degree is accounted for in just a word—"successfully construct," "accurately describe"—but in such cases, be prepared to set criteria for successfully and accurately. Sometimes the degree is specific: "list all 12 moving parts," "to within 1/32 inches." As with the condition, the degree is not always stated or required.

**Example: Degree Characteristic Adds Criteria**

In the previous example of adding conditions to learning objectives, we developed three solid objectives that provide clear direction to both students and instructors:

- Students will be able to create and produce a nonverbal performance incorporating various physical movement techniques.
- Students will be able to write feature articles using information gathered from personal interviews.
- After studying a mock crime scene for 60 seconds, students will be able to describe their observations.

These objectives can be sharpened even further by adding a degree of acceptable performance.

- Students will be able to create and produce **a 10-minute** nonverbal performance incorporating **at least three** of the physical movement techniques discussed in class.
- Students will be able to write feature articles, **of**

**500 to 750 words**, using information gathered from personal interviews.

- After studying a mock crime scene for 60 seconds, students will be able to describe their observations, **identifying at least 10 pieces of evidence**.

Stating criteria in the learning objectives helps students to focus their learning efforts and aids you in assessing their performance.

If you state the degree of acceptable performance in your learning objective, be sure it is precise. Criteria such as "to the satisfaction of the instructor," "must be able to make 80 percent on a multiple-choice exam," and "must pass a final exam" are too vague (and in the case of satisfying the instructor, too subjective) to be useful in a learning objective.

The criteria must relate directly to the behavior and provide a means to measure it. Making 80 percent on an exam and passing a final exam are related to test taking, not to a specific behavior stated in a learning objective. "To the satisfaction of the instructor" could be salvaged by changing it to "according to an instructor-supplied checklist of criteria."

**Knowledge Check**

1.  Which part of this objective is an example of a degree? *At the end of this module, instructors will be able to create learning objectives in a standardized format for every component of their online course.*

    a.  "Create learning objectives in a standardized format"

    b.  "At the end of this module"

    c.  "Instructors"

    d.  This learning objective does not contain a degree.

    e.  "Every component of their online course"

Answers:

1. e: "Every component of their online course" is the degree.

# WRITING LEARNING OBJECTIVES

# REALIZING THE FULL POWER OF LEARNING OBJECTIVES

Virtually all instructors have learning objectives in mind when developing a course. They know the skills and knowledge that students should gain by the end of each instructional unit. However, many instructors are not in the habit of writing learning objectives, and the objectives remain implicit. The full power of learning objectives is realized only when the learning objectives are explicitly stated. Writing clear learning objectives is therefore a critical skill.

To sharpen this skill so that your objectives are consistently precise, measurable, and student-centered, we recommend that you follow the audience, behavior, condition, degree (ABCD) method. Every learning objective must have an audience and a stated behavior. The condition and degree are not applicable to every learning objective, but they can make your objectives more precise as long as they are not forced into place.

# AUDIENCE

The important point of the audience characteristic is to understand your audience so that you can make the learning objective student centered. A student-centered objective is aimed at what students must do to demonstrate mastery of a skill, not at what instructors must do to teach the skill.

The audience is generally referred to as "learners," "students," or "participants" but is sometimes addressed in the second person ("you"). It may also be more specific, depending on the course of study or level of education—for example, the audience may be addressed as "massage therapists" or "postdoctoral scholars." Often, the audience element is captured in an introductory sentence such as "Participants will be able to do the following:" preceding a list of objectives.

# BEHAVIOR

An objective clearly states what knowledge or skill a learner is expected to be able to perform. Because the behavior must be observable and/or measurable, action verbs are used. If the behavior were stated as "learners will be able to understand the extraocular muscles and their actions," it would not be an observable or measurable action because understand is intangible.

Bloom's taxonomy and its associated action verbs can help you write learning objectives that describe observable and/or measurable behavior, which is essential to assessing how well the objective is mastered. The domains of Bloom's taxonomy also help you ensure your learning objectives target the level of performance that appropriately demonstrates achievement of the objective. The levels within each domain are categorized along a continuum of cognitive complexity from lower-order to higher-order thinking skills.

- **Cognitive**
  - The cognitive domain addresses knowledge and thinking skills. The six levels of the cognitive domain are remember, understand, apply, analyze, evaluate, and create.
- **Psychomotor**
  - The psychomotor domain encompasses physical skills such as manipulating a tool or an instrument. The four levels of the psychomotor domain are observe, imitate, practice, and adapt.
- **Affective**
  - The affective domain is concerned with subject-

ive areas such as emotional development and conflict resolution. The five levels of the affective domain are receive, respond, value, organize, and characterize (or internalize).

# CONDITION

An objective describes the important conditions (if any) under which the performance is to occur. Example conditions include "working with a partner," "without the use of a calculator," and "given a CPR manikin." Note that "after completing this course" does not constitute a condition.

# DEGREE

Wherever possible, an objective describes the criterion of acceptable performance. The degree might be expressed in terms such as "list 200 of the 206 human bones," "in 25 or fewer words," or "with 80 percent accuracy." In many learning objectives, the degree is implicit; "without error," for example, can be assumed unless a different criterion is explicitly stated.

# USING CLEAR LANGUAGE

When writing learning objectives, keep your language clear and simple, and avoid using buzzwords and abbreviations. Students are unlikely to be familiar with education jargon ("ed-speak"), and jargon has a tendency to change quickly. For example, students learning English as a second language once were known as LEP (limited English proficient) students. Now they are called ELLs (English language learners).

Another way to keep your learning objectives clear is to avoid words and phrases that may clutter your writing and translate to gibberish. Mager (1999) provides the following examples of gibberish to be avoided:

- Manifest an increasing comprehensive understanding
- Demonstrate a thorough comprehension
- Relate and foster with multiple approaches
- Have a deep awareness and thorough humanizing grasp

When you find phrases such as these, rewrite them in terms that students cannot misinterpret.

**Knowledge Check**

1.  Look at the following objective and identify which of the ABCD elements are included. Select all

that apply. *Students should be able to communicate with team members in order to manage time effectively to provide appropriate evidence-based care.*

    a.   Audience
    b.   Behavior
    c.   Condition
    d.   Degree

2.   Read the following sentence and identify which characteristics of the ABCDs, if any, must be improved to make it an effective objective. Select all that apply. *Wherever possible, further develop my knowledge and skills in order to provide effective, evidenced-based nursing care for the duration of the patient visit.*

    a.   Audience
    b.   Behavior
    c.   Condition
    d.   Degree

3.   Which of the following characteristics from the ABCD method are critical to writing a student-centered and observable and/or measurable objective? Select all that apply.

    a.   Audience
    b.   Behavior
    c.   Condition
    d.   Degree

4.   Which of the following learning objectives best incorporates all four of the ABCD characteristics of a well-written objective?

    a.   Classify a data analysis situation (involving two variables) according to the "role-type classification," and state the appropriate display and/or numerical measures that should be used to summarize the data with a rubric score of 3 (out of 5) or better.
    b.   Graphically display the relationship

between two quantitative variables and describe (a) the overall pattern and (b) striking deviations from the pattern.

c.   Interpret the value of the correlation coefficient, and be aware of its limitations as a numerical measure of the association between two quantitative variables.

d.   Apply probability rules to find the likelihood of an event.

5.   Which of the following ABCD characteristics is most problematic in this example? *Students will be acquainted with using all of the characteristics described in the ABCD method.*

a.   Audience
b.   Behavior
c.   Condition
d.   Degree

Answers:

1.   Audience and Behavior: This learning objective contains the audience element (students) and the behavior element (communicate).

2.   Audience, Behavior, Condition, Degree: The audience is not stated in the objective, but it is implied by the word "my," which means this objective is not student centered and is consequently flawed. "Develop knowledge and skills and provide effective care" are behaviors that are difficult to observe and/or measure, so the verbs describing the behaviors must be changed to make this statement an effective learning objective. The duration of a patient visit is not a condition. This objective contains no degree, which, as we have mentioned, is not always necessary.

3.   Audience and Behavior: Objectives need an audience to be student centered and a behavior to be observable and/or measurable.

4.   a: This objective contains an audience (students), behaviors (classify and state), a condition (according to the "role-type classification"), and a degree (3 out of 5).

5.   b: The phrase "acquainted with" is problematic because a student's ability to be acquainted with a concept would be difficult to observe or measure.

# CONSIDERATIONS IN WRITING LEARNING OBJECTIVES

# SUFFICIENT BREADTH AND SCOPE OF LEARNING OBJECTIVES

Learning objectives don't come in one-size-fits-all. Some are broad and encompassing; others are small and specific. Their breadth and scope depend in part on the level of your course and sophistication of your students. They also depend on the instructional unit for which they are written: learning objectives written for an overall course are broad, whereas those written for a module within the course are narrower, and those written for a component with the module are narrower still. The following table can help you determine whether your learning objectives are appropriately scoped and provides a few strategies for adjusting their size.

| Too Big | Too Small |
|---|---|
| *Do your objectives sound generic, as though they could appear on a syllabus in almost any course or discipline?* | *Do your objectives contain repetition and overlap?* |
| Try to make your objectives specific to your course and discipline. For example, the objective: | If so, you may be able to combine some of these objectives. For example, |
| <ul><li>Apply the principles and concepts from this course to solve real-world problems.</li></ul> | <ul><li>Describe the tenets of functionalism</li><li>Describe the tenets of structuralism</li><li>Describe the tenets of postmodernism</li></ul> |
| This could apply to numerous disciplines, think what it means for yours. Changing the objective to: | These three objectives could be collapsed to become "Describe the tenets of major theoretical orientations in anthropology." |
| <ul><li>Apply the principles of optimization and elasticity to solve basic economics problems.</li></ul> | |
| This makes it specific and unambiguous. | |

*Could your objectives describe an entire curriculum?*

It is a worthy goal for students to be able to "think like a research biologist," but that is too ambitious an objective for a single course. If your objectives are similarly broad, break them down into component skills, and ask yourself what students will learn in this *one* course that will contribute to this broader goal.

*Do your objectives read like the task specifications for an assignment?*

Try identifying the larger skill you want students to attain. For example, the objective

- Students should be able to write a 4- to 5-page paper that explains the relationship between theory X and theory Y.

might become

- Explain the relationships among theories of child development.

# SUFFICIENT NUMBER
# OF LEARNING
# OBJECTIVES

An entire discipline cannot be taught in a single semester, so you must be selective about the material you include in your course. Too many learning objectives translates to too much instructional content, limiting the time you can spend on each objective and overwhelming both you and your students. Conversely, too few objectives can lead to a shallow course that does not prepare students for the next step in their education.

There is no right number of learning objectives for a course. The range of objectives in a course are wide because every course is different in size and scope. Consequently, developing the right number of learning objectives is not a question of deciding how many you should have; it's a question of how many best support your course goals.

If you feel the number of learning objectives is getting too high, you should prioritize them according to the most important takeaways for students. Also, look for repetition in the objectives —you may be able to combine some of them. Finally, look for overly ambitious objectives that can be omitted without sacrificing the quality of instruction.

If you find you have too few learning objectives, check whether they are too high-level or too vague in specifying the skills and knowledge you want students to gain. They can probably be broken out into two or more objectives.

# BEFORE YOU START WRITING

Before you start writing your learning objectives, here are a few points to keep in mind.

Developing learning objectives is

- **A time-consuming process**: It takes careful thought and revision to produce a polished set of learning objectives. Allow yourself plenty of time for this task.

- **An iterative process**: Learning objectives provide the foundation for designing your course, but once they are written, expect to revise and refine the objectives to keep them in alignment with your content, activities, and assessments.

- **A flexible process**: You can find helpful tips and guidelines for developing effective learning objectives, but you will not find rigid rules. You (and your team if you work with one) must be flexible as you create objectives that work best for your course.

# REFERENCES

Anderson, L. W., and Krathwohl, D. R. (Ed.). 2001. *A Taxonomy for Learning, Teaching, and Assessing: A Revision of Bloom's Taxonomy of Educational Objectives* [complete edition]. New York: Longman.

Bloom, B. S. 1956. Taxonomy of Educational Objectives, Handbook I: The Cognitive Domain. New York: David McKay Co.

Bloom, B., Engelhart, M., Furst, E., Hill, W., & Krathwohl, D. (1974). Taxonomy of educational objectives: The classification of educational goals. (B. Bloom, Ed.). New York: David McKay Co., Inc.

Georgia State University (1999). Mager's Tips on Instructional Objectives. Adapted from Mager, R. F., 1984, Preparing Instructional Objectives (2nd ed.). Belmont, CA: David S. Lake.

Krathwohl DR. 2002. A revision of Bloom's taxonomy: An overview. Theory Practice, 41:212–218.

---

[1] Bloom, B., Engelhart, M., Furst, E., Hill, W., & Krathwohl, D. (1974). Taxonomy of educational objectives: The classification of educational goals. (B. Bloom, Ed.). New York: David McKay Co., Inc.

[2] Bloom, B. S. 1956. Taxonomy of Educational Objectives, Handbook I: The Cognitive Domain. New York: David McKay Co.

[3] Anderson, L. W., and Krathwohl, D. R. (Ed.). 2001. A Taxonomy for Learning, Teaching, and Assessing: A Revision of Bloom's Taxonomy of Educational Objectives [complete edition]. New York: Longman.

[4] Krathwohl DR. 2002. A revision of Bloom's taxonomy: An overview.

Theory Practice, 41:212–218.

[5] Bloom, B. S. 1956. Taxonomy of Educational Objectives, Handbook I: The Cognitive Domain. New York: David McKay Co.

[6] Anderson, L. W., and Krathwohl, D. R. (Ed.). 2001. A Taxonomy for Learning, Teaching, and Assessing: A Revision of Bloom's Taxonomy of Educational Objectives [complete edition]. New York: Longman.

Made in the USA
Middletown, DE
05 July 2021